Read Aloud
Animal Stories 5
For Families

It Takes All Kinds

Collected by
Claire Suminski &
Henrietta S. Haithcock

Illustrated by Susan Swedlund and Friends

A special thank you to our artists Julia Stanley and Sue Brown, and photographers Libby Weber and Cheryl Binnall.

Copyright 2024 by Claire Suminski

All rights reserved.

No part of this book may be used or reproduced in any manner whatsoever without written permission. Contact Suminski Family Books, 186 Jim Berry Road, Franklin, NC 28734

First Edition
ISBN 979-8-9856781-8-5

Published by Suminski Family Books

suminskifamilybooks.com

The Animals of Brendle Road	1
The Full Moon Opossum Porch Party	7
A Bear Makes Friends	9
South Seas Rhincodon Typus Anyone?	13
This Donkey is "For Sale"!	17
The Path to Friendship	18
Shanay, the Wonder Dog	22
At Home with the Lake Emory Eagles	29
Lasting Memories of Merry and Bounty	33
My Eagle Watching Journey: "Fly Eagles Fly"	35
An Eagle Love Story	37

Articles, Games and Puzzles

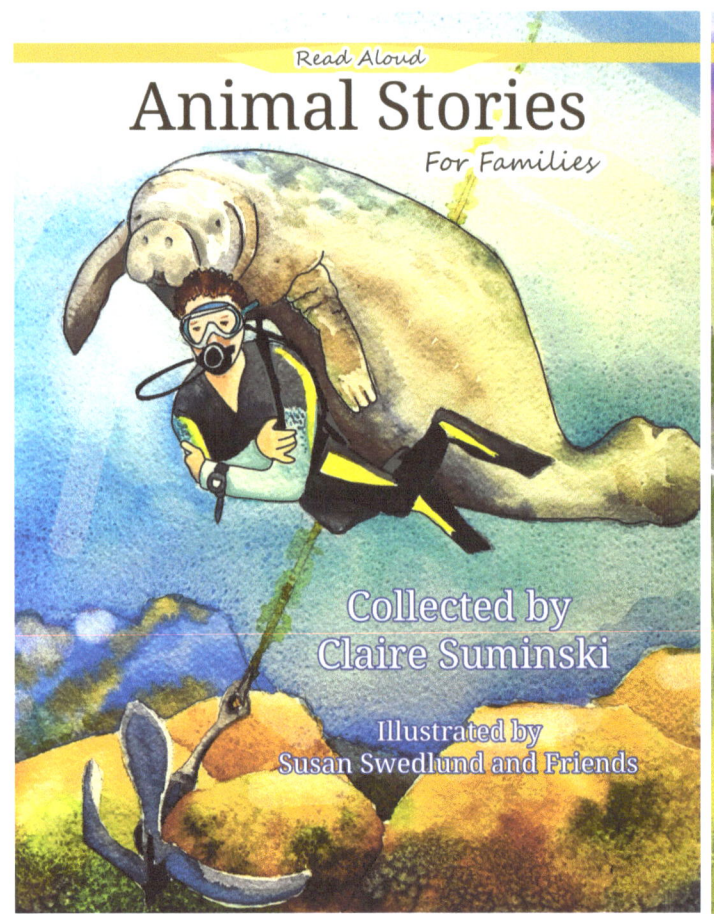
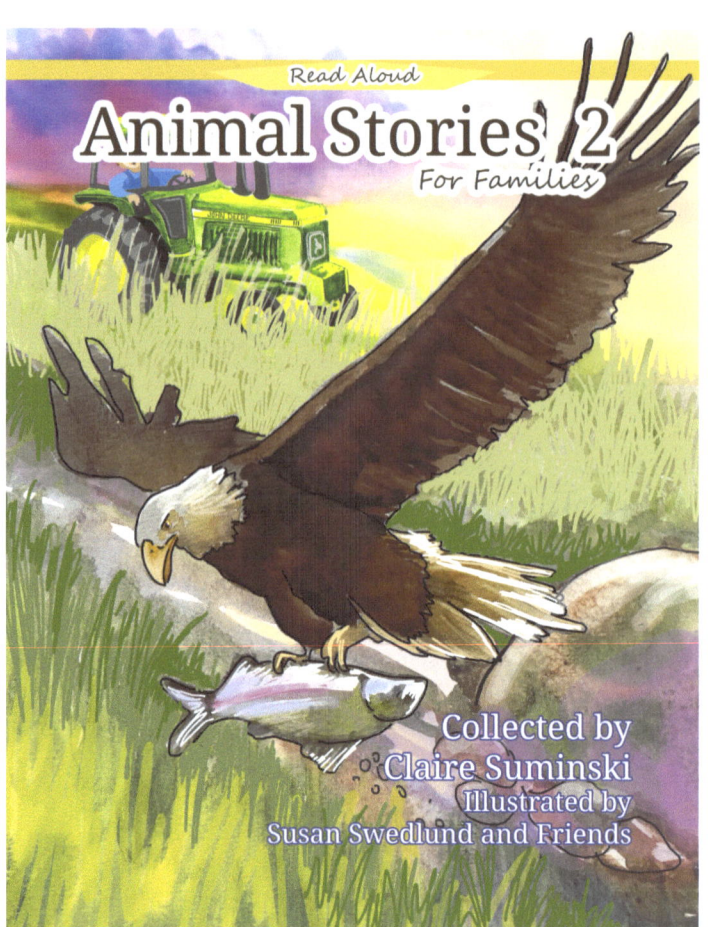
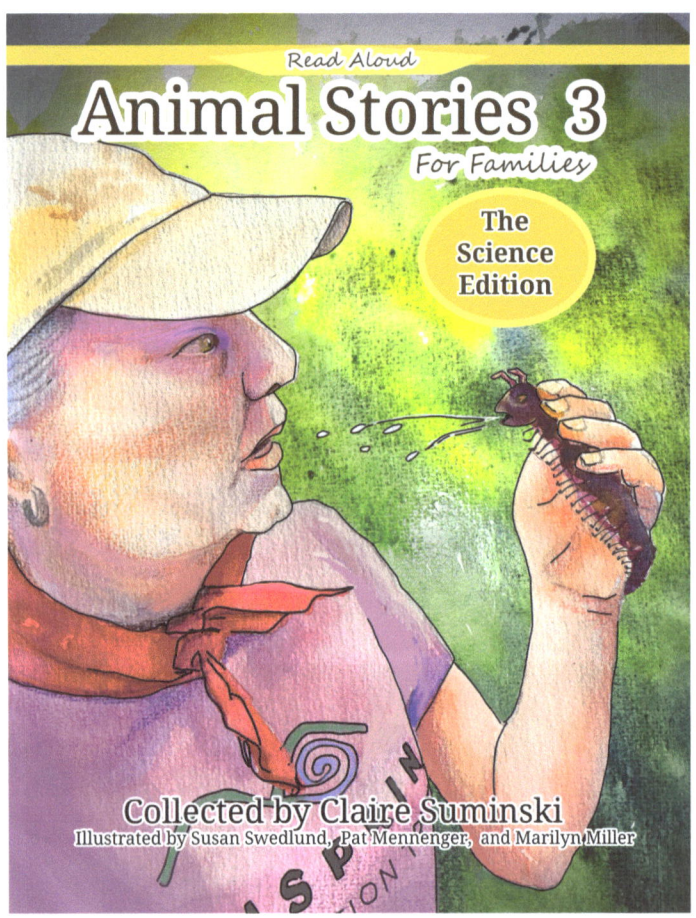

suminskifamilybooks.com

The Animals of Brendle Road

Recollections from Donna Barlow as told to Claire Suminski

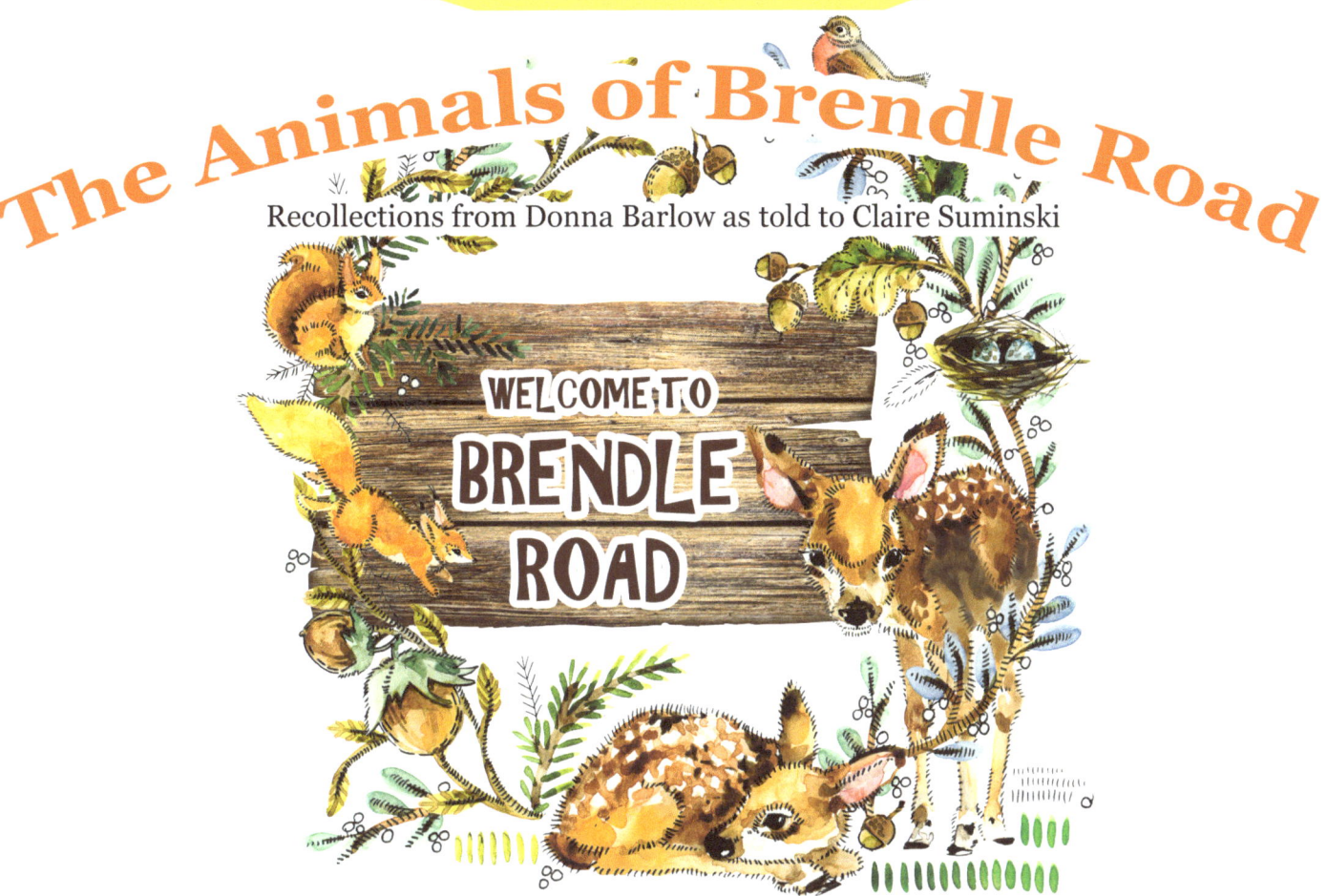

When I was growing up, animals of all kinds added quite a bit of spice to our lives. There was a steady flow of domesticated animals: cats, Guinea Fowl, chickens and even a few horses for which we were responsible. It seemed like the Guinea Fowl were always chasing and pecking at us and we found them very annoying. We depended on the chickens for eggs and meat, but cats were our favorite animals. They would keep down the mouse population, and we loved playing with them. Some of the horses were trained, others barely broke. One time my Daddy went to the livestock auction and came home with two beautiful young female horses for my sister and I to ride. I climbed up on one filly to ride around the yard and she took off running , heading right for a clothes line full of freshly washed linens. I barely escaped disaster and decided from then on to proceed with caution when riding auction horses!

There was a lot of wildlife on our road as well. Foxes, possums, racoons, snakes, mice, bobcats, bears and even panthers all passed through our neighborhood at one time or another. Brendle Road is a U-shaped holler with steep hillsides on three sides. Lively Coon Creek rushes and turns its way downward from high up on Cowee Mountain. Animals and people had to find ways to co-exist on Brendle Road.

Animal Stories

It was common for families to hunt, fish, garden, raise animals and put up food. So much of our lives revolved around the canning house and the smoke house. My family had two big gardens and my maternal grandmother, Mamaw Sanders, worked hard at putting up fruits, vegetables and homemade soups, which we enjoyed all year long, especially during cold, snowy winters when we couldn't get to Shorty Mason's Food Palace. We always had food to eat. But the best part of the canning house, was that Papaw John made an area up in the canning house eaves for the mama cats to give birth to their kittens. There was a ramp leading up to a little hole just big enough for mama to get in and out and take care of her kittens. When the proud mama cat was good and ready, she would lead them down that ramp for all of us to admire. My sisters and I would get so excited and would enjoy weeks of playing with those kittens. One time an orange tabby led three fluffy orange fur balls down the ramp, and we were squealing with delight. This way of living brought us the kind of happiness that money cannot buy!

Animal Stories

Animal Stories

By our gardens was a big ol' apple tree. With a thick, long branch that hung over a side road. Apple sauce, apple cake, apple pie and more delicious food came from the apples we harvested from that tree. The wild animals thought those apples were delicious, too!

One day we went out to the garden and there was a big ol' bear asleep in that apple tree. Imagine that! The bear had stretched out on that branch with all four limbs hanging down. He had stuffed himself with apples to the point that he could barely move and had laid down on that branch, in order to sleep off his apple-drunk state. We called the forest service and a ranger came right away and tranquillized the bear and loaded him into the Forest Service trunk. While the bear was fast sleep the ranger let my sisters and I pet the bear and look him over real good. This is something that they would not allow today. But we loved it. Good thing that bear did not wake up early!

Animal Stories

When I was older, I got a job at Hickory Ranch Restaurant and drove myself back and forth to work. My family regularly heard a panther crying out at night, from up the holler, just above our house. I was nervous that it might try and chase me when I came home after work. This was during the days of no air conditioning. We would keep our windows open while we slept in order to stay cool. I asked my Daddy if I could park my car right next to the house. I would jump out and run in the house as fast as I could, with my heart beating fast. Well, one night, I ran in the house and into my bedroom and could hear the panther screaming right outside my window screen! It was hotter than blazes, but I shut that window and slept in a hot room that night!

A couple of nights later, my Mama called me out to the front porch and there was that panther in the middle of Brendle Road. He was dragging and scratching his claws on the road and we could see just how big he was. He was grey and about 6 feet long with a long tail another 3 feet long. My mother stood on the porch, mesmerized. And then I heard my Daddy yell, "Get in the house NOW!!!" Authorities say that panthers no longer live in Macon County. But sometimes we catch a glimpse of one coming down through the holler or crossing an old country road. Thankfully, that big grey one from years ago never did try and get me. However, he did become a folk legend in my family and is part of my memories of the animals of Brendle Road.

Animal Stories

Illustration by Ros Webb

The Full Moon Opossum Porch Party

by Claire Suminski

Coweeta (WeeTee), our farm cat, loves to roam around the farm at night helping Cowee Sam keep our flock of poultry safe from wandering vermin looking for a chicken dinner. Only with the threat of extreme weather coming does she ask to come inside and spend the night.

Morning is a different story. WeeTee is "up and at 'em" before the sun has peeked over the horizon. As soon as she hears me in the kitchen, she puts in her breakfast order with musical meow tones, rattles, and bumps. We usually have a very pleasant conversation, and she receives several pats and neck scratches as I fix her gourmet cat food exactly the way she likes it, with a wee bit of water to make a gravy.

Funny thing about our cat is that she will be hooked on one kind of cat food for weeks and then suddenly turn up her nose and refuse to eat it. I really have to be on my toes with Wee Tee. We had just gone through a dark valley of feline culinary dissatisfaction, resulting in me trying out several new brands of cat food. When I found one that she would eat, I ran to the store and purchased the biggest bag of that brand they had! When I got it home, the amount was too big to fit in the cat food storage container, which has bricks stacked on top of it to make it as tight as Fort Knox! After filling the secure container as high as I could, I rolled down the top of the bag to keep the remaining food fresh. The moon was full and glowing as I went back into the house to curl up in my cozy bed for a good night's sleep.

We have a student size mini fridge just outside the front door that comes about waist high. Just before daybreak, I thought I heard Wee Tee on the porch and threw open the door to say hello. There she was, on top of the mini fridge, and I reached out to give her a little scratch. All of a sudden, there was a hissing, growling sound, and I quickly stepped backwards, realizing this could not be Wee Tee! It was a rather large Opposum!

I was making my own kind of funny noises, too. I yelled out of surprise and shook my head, as I tried to shoe the opossum off the porch. I flipped on the porch light and surprise, surprise, there seemed to be baby possums running every which way!

Not wanting to be separated from their mama opossum, they were scurrying after her. The big bag of cat food was torn open, resulting in food being scattered everywhere! I had interrupted an opossum porch party!

The Full Moon Opossum Porch Party!

As the full moon rises in the soft autumn sky,
The racoons and opossums no longer seem shy.
Travelling country roads and up hill and dale,
From persimmons to garbage,
They munch along the trail.

So, lock up your cat food and other delights,
Or the racoons & opossums might give you a fright!
Travelling country roads and up hill and dale,
From persimmons to garbage,
They munch along the trail.

Animal Stories

A Bear Makes Friends

A true story by
Henrietta S. Haithcock

A family hiking outing on Beehive Basin in Montana, and even on trails in Yellowstone National Park never placed us in the path of any kind of BEAR. Maybe the size of our group as we talked, sang, and jingled bells alerted the bear to our presence, and they wanted no part of us. But... On another hiking adventure in Gatlinburg, Tennessee on the Rainbow Falls Trail, a true black bear experience awaited.

Jaunting along the trail with my husband, Pete, my daughter, Molly, and her friend, Tiffany, we were thrilled beyond measure to be out and about in nature on a beautiful spring day. Excited and full of energy would be a perfect description for the two middle grade kids. Feeling guilty that I had teased and unnerved them about meeting a bear on the trail, I decided to make amends. Instructing the two girls on bear protocol, in the unlikely event they might face a hairy beast. I never dreamed our hike would become a quest for survival, well maybe not that serious. But it could have been!

The walk along the trail was dazzling with wildflowers blooming profusely: lady's slippers, jack-in-the-pulpit, trillium, trout lilies, blood root, azalea, rhododendron, and mountain laurel. The shaded setting of the forest brought a tranquil aura to this endless expanse of the mountain forest home. Fern fronds were unfurling over the forest floor, appearing to create a lush green carpet for the animals. The overall hike was uneventful, except for the sighting of a deer roaming by the stream to the right of the trail.

Animal Stories

Animal Stories

The children skipped along the trail in total abandonment as they innocently meandered safely beyond the thrilling event about to take place. No slowing down, no siree! I, on the other hand, taking calculated steps with my hiking stick to curtail the event of a fall, became a lone hiker in the sunless canopy of the trees.

The trail was crowded with roots crawling over the path, intertwining and tripping even the most seasoned hikers with their knotted, spreading fingers. Meticulously stepping around and over the obstacle of roots, rocks, and boulders, I began to fall farther and farther behind, and no one waited for me. My new nickname became "Cow's Tail."

Happily traversing along the trail, I experienced the sights and sounds of a living forest: bird, deer, groundhog, and squirrel. The thought of a bear encounter was a million miles away in my imagination. Maybe it would serve me right to meet a burly beast after all my teasing with the girls.

Later in the afternoon, ambling at a slower pace, the rigors of the walk soon made me want to take a short rest. Leaning my full weight on the walking stick, I glanced up, and what I saw shocked me into a frozen trance. I had forgotten who the true keeper of the forest was. Out of the blue, a humongous 500-hundred-pound black bear casually and gracefully jumped off the embankment to the left of the trail. He landed about 30 feet directly in front of me. I couldn't think, move, or breathe. Frozen in time, my mind went blank.

Our eyes locked! An eternity passed before the transition between time and space released us. Bears are territorial by nature. This bear made his own rules, and finally decided that I was not such a scary human. He jumped off the trail down into a riverbed without another glance toward me. Yikes! My brain thawed! That bear had granted me another day to play on God's green earth. "Yes, I was thankful," my brain slowly informed me.

Animal Stories

   A group of students from the University of Tennessee had been hiking some distance behind me and happened to close the gap between us, witnessing the entire event. Rushing forward, they began to excitedly express themselves in a foreign language. Pointing to their camera, they had taken photos and were extremely proud.

   A few minutes later, my family came running back down the trail to check on "Cow's Tail", and the story became a legend- *Bear makes friends… from a distance!*

Animal Stories

South Seas Rhincodon Typus Anyone?

By Claire Suminski

Mikal works as a tour guide on the Caribbean Island of Aruba, off the coast of Venezuela. Even though he enjoys the restaurants and other amenities found on this lovely island, he is equally at home eating off the land. Iguanas are found in abundance and grow to be over 5 feet long. When Iguanas are cooked in the right way, they taste like a very tender chicken. Cactus plants also abound. They bear fruit that is very popular, and he enjoys eating them as well.

When Mikal was in his teens, he and his friends loved to go snorkeling out by a coral reef. One day when they were out by the reef swimming, things were very calm and quiet, which he very much enjoyed. Suddenly, the very colorful fish populating the reef began to disperse and leave the reef. Mikal and his friends quickly surveyed the area to see if a predator was nearby. They saw nothing, but his friend gave the hand signal for them to get out of the water. Just then, Mikal turned his head to the left and less than a foot away from him was a fish that appeared to be bigger than a bus!

He could have reached out and touched this animal. Like in a cartoon, his arms and legs were moving, but everything was in slow motion. Mikal said that his whole young life flashed before him.

He wondered if this fish was going to eat him for dinner! The fish did not try to eat him, and as his heartrate slowed, Mikal noticed the black and white spots common to whale sharks. Whale sharks (Rhincodon Typus) are slow-moving, filter-feeding fish, that can grow to be over 40 feet long and weigh over 20 tons! They eat plankton, not people. He was safe!

Animal Stories

Years later, Mikal found a job driving a bus and telling his stories to tourists making port calls in Aruba. This real story from his life in Aruba has ended up being a crowd-pleaser. I know because I was a passenger on his bus! At certain times of year, whale sharks pass through the area he snorkels in. But this is the only time a South Seas Rhincodon, about as big as his bus, pulled up and parked right next to him!

Animal Stories

Animal Stories

This Donkey is "For Sale"!

Written by Claire Suminski
Illustrated by Sue Brown

Before Cowee Mountain Valley Farm took on Sam as guardian of all of the goats, pigs and chickens, Farmer Joe thought he might try a guardian donkey. The Tallent family, owners of our nearby farm stand, used guardian donkeys very successfully to watch over their cattle. Two foals had been born a few months back and they offered to sell us one for $125. They dropped the foal off in our pasture. She must have missed her family so much! We wanted to pet her and comfort her and give her treats. But, she was afraid and would not let any humans come close to her.

Farmer Joe said, "Hmmmm, we will just have to see how she does." We were having a huge predator problem; mostly foxes trying to get the chickens. They were picking off our prized hens on a regular basis. It was soon evident that our little donkey foal did not know what to do! The kids and I were sympathetic to her plight. One morning Farmer Joe went out to take care of the farm animals and found a dead chicken with a big donkey poop right next to it!

"This little donkey has had her chance!" said Farmer Joe, "However, pooping next to a dead chicken is not the answer! I am selling her!" The rest of the family was trying to tame this little foal, and of course, we were attached. Joe was a volunteer fireman and knew many farmers in our small mountain community. It did not take him long to find a buyer... for $25! Oh no! What to do? The rest of the family wanted this donkey foal to stay. Being the manager of the family finances and a homeschool math Mom, I countered, "But dear, that is a $100 loss!" He replied, "Oh don't you worry, my dear, I can find a buyer who will pay full price for this donkey, who I have officially named "For Sale". He could see that I just did not want to see our foal go, but on a farm, every animal needs to pull its own weight.

The next day, a deal was struck with the UPS driver, who raised cattle on the side and had other guardian donkeys on his farm. I checked back with him a few weeks later and he said that For Sale was doing her part to protect the heifer calves and steer calves from coyotes. We missed her, but she had found a place where she was useful and could learn from the other donkeys. For Sale's departure, although sad, opened the door for us to welcome in a new member to the barnyard family, that would change our lives in so many ways... Cowee Sam!

Animal Stories

THE PATH TO FRIENDSHIP

A story shared by Ashley Hoover and Vicki Cole;
written by Henrietta S. Haithcock
Illustrated by Sue Brown

Sometimes in life, endearing stories emerge from our memory caches, and the stories about friendship are always the best. This is the story of a young child and a palomino horse that form an unlikely bond, taking place over a period of five years in the Louisa Chapel Community on Scroggs Road.

Estella was only eighteen months old when she went on her first real walk down Scroggs Road with Mom Ashley and Mimi Vickie. Being the happy little girl that she was, going outside to explore and play filled her with exuberant joy. Little Estella loved nature's flora and fauna: bright summer flowers, soft green grass, caterpillars and butterflies, to name a few. Nothing was safe from her grasp! Estella would laugh and run as fast as her little legs could carry her. It was not easy keeping up with this little one. She was a blond-haired, blue-eyed bundle of joy. And she was always seen strolling in her favorite color— pink.

Estella was brimming over with the kind of energy that radiates to everyone around her. Her enthusiasm for life made Mom's and Mimi's world much brighter and filled with love.

On one exceptionally pleasant morning, Mom said, "What would you like to do today, Estella?" Estella's tiny hand pointed toward the door. Understanding, Mom said," It is a beautiful day for a stroll in our mountains, Estella. Let's go exploring and find a new adventure." On this particular day, strolling down their road, mother and child saw two horses trotting around a small fenced in pasture. One of the horses seemed especially bold— a palomino. She seemed to be a friendly mare and slowly approached the fence. Strikingly handsome would describe her golden colored coat and light cream mane and tail.

Animal Stories

There was nothing at all menacing about the horse's approach as she trotted expectantly toward Estella and Mom. She must have thought that they had a treat for her—an apple or a carrot. CRIES and SHRIEKS! Mom was shocked to hear the panic-stricken outbursts coming from her child's wide-open mouth. Estella became hysterical and continued the ear-piercing screams of uncontrollable fear. Clutching her mom for assurance and safety, she must have perceived this enormous animal as a threat to her small world. It was awful! Poor Mother! They turned around and hurried home.

Animal Stories

After this first initiation, Mom and Mimi tried to comfort little Estella and showed her picture books with horses. Mom explained to her child that they had met a new friend that day—a palomino horse. Mom and Mimi decided to help her name their new friend. Estella called her *Yellow Horse*.

So young and so inquisitive, learning from safe arms and loving assurance, Estella would outgrow her fear of horses. Someday, that fear turn into sheer joy at the sight of this gentle, magnificent animal. Each day and every walk down Scrogg's Road rolled by into a succession of about five years. An eighteen-month-old grew into a toddler and then into a kindergarten child— a big girl! At first, Estella would sit and watch Yellow Horse at a safe distance from the fence. Slowly, each meeting with Yellow Horse brought a sense of wonder as she began to approach the horse without fear and trepidation. "You can pet her, feed her a treat, and show her that you love her," said Mimi. By showing her love, she will become confident and trust you. Now you and Yellow Horse can become true friends.

And it's true that over time, Estella became more and more comfortable as Yellow Horse approached the old, weathered fence. Estella began to pat the horse's head. On another visit, she held out her hand filled with grass for Yellow Horse, and she gently ate it. The next step toward friendship with the palomino became evident when Estella began talking to the horse, and the horse whinnied an approval back. Another sweet moment was experienced when Estella introduced her doll to Yellow Horse.

Animal Stories

The "icing on the cake" happened quite unexpectedly one afternoon, as Penny and Estella pressed their foreheads together through the fence. A bond was shared. Forever bonds can be created between animals and people, especially little people. Kindness and trust are keys to successful relationships, a unique understanding that knows no limits for faithful friends.

Animal Stories

Shanay, the Wonder Dog
by Henrietta S. Haithcock

This is a wonder dog tale about the blessing our family received one happy Christmas morning: a Golden Labrador pup looking smart in a bright red bow. She greeted us every morning after with wet kisses for fifteen years. Shanay's breed blended a dog with super canine smarts and a loving personality. This rollie pollie ball of yellow fur would grow up to rule our household as a delightful companion and devoted protector. Over the years, she became a sort of dog nanny to the children. Here are the adventures of our dog, Shanay, shared as her own personal memoirs.

Firm hands gently placed me between two little girls where I nestled against their warm bodies under some heavy covers called quilts. It was dark. I was not scared because I already had a sense of belonging that made me whimper with pure joy long into the night. Before dozing off, I heard the faint echo of heavy boot steps, deep chuckling, and jingling bells from somewhere far off. I had arrived in the wee hours of Christmas morning! Sporting a red bow made me adorable. My new family cuddled and patiently helped me to learn my name, Shanay, meaning "beautiful eyes."

I was instantly devoted to my people. The biggest mission in my doggie life was set from the start: keeping my family safe. A life-long love of protecting was exciting yet challenging each and every day. There was always some new danger my people were creating for themselves. With dog senses as keen and sharp as mine, it would have been impossible for me to quit my job. It was also impossible to train them. Nothing else mattered so much to me for the rest of my life.

We frequently went on summer day trips to Chatuge Lake in Hiawassee, Georgia. I was always fashionably dressed in my favorite blue halter. My pet peeve was being leashed to our picnic table. Why could I not run down to the water with them? I tried to make them understand by barking, but my anguished cries were rudely ignored. I persisted with my howling, "UNFAIR!"

As we all know, my Lab breed loves to swim. I was a water freak and would greet the water with gusto, diving out into the deeper water to retrieve any object, no matter how large. Fishing out balls and sticks was my specialty— the small stuff.

Finally, the joyful shrieks and splashing sounds of my people made me come undone. Wriggling with determination, I became Houdini doggie and pulled right out of my halter, howling, "Yeehaw!" I felt the adrenalin of freedom and bolted to the shoreline. Quietly, I slipped into the water. Swish! Swish! I liked to sneak up on them, swimming doggie-paddle style.

My people were having such fun diving and dunking each other under the water; they did not see me swimming toward them. Catherine, the oldest child, thought it would be great sport to tease this vigilant dog. She would yell, "Help!" while dramatically thrusting her arms up toward the cloudless sky. She would then slowly sink beneath the waves. My "rescue dog" signal flashed in my brain, and I had to follow my instincts. I desperately paddled to her, gently grabbed a mouthful of ponytail in my teeth, and kicked hard to the shore with a purpose. Unfortunately, any other family members in the underwater vicinity felt the love with my toenail scratches all over their exposed bodies.

Fellow swimmers and sunbathers were clapping and cheering me on. For me, though, it was just part of the rescue deal I had made with my people long ago. Suddenly, I was so tired and felt like dropping to the ground. After a long, sunny day of excitement and my mission being completed, I didn't mind jumping into our Big Happy Van, curling up, and enjoying the sweetest dreams all the way home.

Animal Stories

Backyards in the mountains can be full of unexpected surprises. Turn your head and a big, black furry critter could be glanced— in a flash— in the corner of your eye. I learned to be on guard for anything.

Two sisters picnicking one summer afternoon were witnesses to such an unexpected event. Having full tummies, the warm breeze and soft sunlight filtering through the pine tree forest made all the right conditions for a perfect afternoon. Stretched out on the blanket, unaware of danger, the girls closed their eyes. Crack! Crunch! Suddenly, out of nowhere, a burly critter bounded out of the serene setting of the pine trees. Alerted by screams, I raced across the picnic blanket, scattering cookies and sandwiches in an instant flurry. With fierce barks and deep growls, I chased the intruder off, letting him know I meant business: defending my people and my territory. All that the girls would later recall was a flash of white teeth and two clashes of fur, one black and one yellow, running through the trees. Could it have been a bear? Yes, they thought as much, but I immediately recognized that distinct odor—BEAR!

Animal Stories

My people loved to play in their backyard every day. It presented big challenges for me. For instance, swing sets and trampolines made me very nervous. On many occasions, I had to participate in their foolish activities just to keep them safe. I must admit that my people were difficult to train.

Remembering the first swing dilemma makes me feel like howling. Mom and Molly would position their legs on the ground and push off, making them fly through the air. This silly action had to be stopped. I discovered that positioning my 89-pound doggie body against their legs made them motionless. Finally understanding my instructions, they gave it up. I knew what was best after all, and I started to believe that Mom was beginning to accept and value my instinctive judgments more and more each day.

Mom and Molly also liked to look silly jumping around in the air on something they called a trampoline. This was not a smart activity in my opinion. Soon they grew tired and lay flat on their backs. I could hear them talking about the funny cloud shapes in the sky. I tried to get their attention, so I poked my nose into Mom's back. She continued to ignore me, and they decided to bounce and jump again. This made my blood boil over with "rescue flash", so I decided to teach them a lesson. Gathering all my strength, I surprised them by jumping onto the trampoline. Whew! My plan was to knock her down and pounce on those legs, which I did. That stopped her! I thought, "Mom should not behave that way." They thought I had gone nutty. Well, I knew what I was about!

Snow days! My favorite! Excited for the long-awaited wintery days of white, my people would pack me into the van and off we would go to the park on our sledding adventure. Watching them slide down the hill, I soon realized that I must not let them crash into a tree or roll off into the nearby river. With each sledding takeoff, I would spring into action by snatching the rope in my mouth. My rescue plan usually succeeded by stopping the speeding sled but created a nasty wipe out and tipsy tumble for the children. My girls' faces would be plastered in the icy hill. I tried it myself one time and found it exhilarating. After all of those brilliant rescue attempts, though, Mom tied me to a tree for the rest of our sledding adventure.

Butterflies and Fontana Lake—this was a boating trip almost gone terribly wrong. One summer afternoon, we had embarked on a breezy boat ride to a new camping adventure in the woods on Fontana Lake. My position on deck was keeping sentry at the front of our pontoon boat. Gazing out into the sparkling lake, I was mesmerized into a state of calm.

All was quiet and peaceful until a butterfly fluttered past my head. I blinked. A black and orange-red Monarch gently lit on my snout. It took me by surprise! I responded swiftly by leaping into the air with eyes and mouth wide open. Kerplunk! Splash! Down, down, down I sank into the water only to be carried underneath the boat between the twin tubes. The motor was roaring at full throttle. I could hear my people screaming as l drifted toward the stern of the boat. "Cut the engine! Cut the engine! Shanay jumped off the front of the boat!" someone screamed at the top of their lungs. Seconds slowly ticked by, and a dodged disaster became a miracle when the motor stopped.

Holding my breath was second nature for me, so the underwater thrill ride was quite refreshing. With all the commotion happening on the surface, though, I felt it was best to pop up. The happy sounds of children's laughter greeted my wet ears as waiting hands caught my water-slogged body. I was safely hauled from the lake into the boat. I did not get a scolding, only hugs. I could not explain my actions, but I really was curious about that butterfly. As fortune would have it, this time, my people rescued me.

Mom's opinion of me ran high. She enjoyed telling other people that there was only one explanation for all of my rescue attempts over the years, "Shanay did not want her people to get hurt. Her intellectual prowess, canine instincts, and protective skills were only matched by her unconditional love for us. She gave us years of beautiful, joy-filled memories. I wish every child could someday be blessed with a dog like Shanay."

Animal Stories

The Lake Emory Eagles

27

Animal Stories

The American Bald Eagle

"Rebuilding the Nest"   Photo by Cheryl Binnall 2024

Notes of Interest:

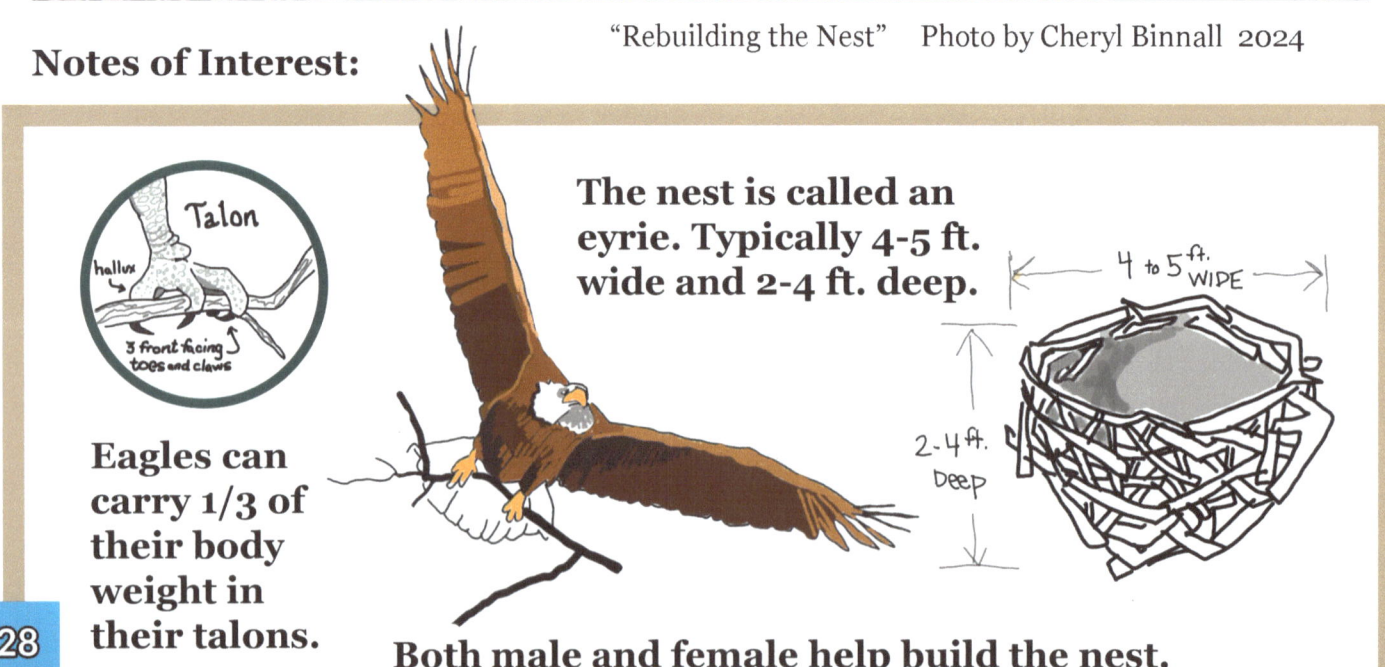

Eagles can carry 1/3 of their body weight in their talons.

The nest is called an eyrie. Typically 4-5 ft. wide and 2-4 ft. deep.

Both male and female help build the nest.

Animal Stories

AT HOME WITH THE LAKE EMORY EAGLES

by Claire Suminski

One of my greatest wildlife adventures has been watching two beautiful American Bald Eagles, America and Bountiful, build a nest and raise a family on our property at the Suminski Farmette. They chose the top section of a pine tree on a point of land reaching into Lake Emory. From 2014 to 2018, before they ever built a nest, Merry and Bounty would stop by to watch for fish from that tree.

Several years ago, five big pines came down in a storm. Pines are notorious for having shallow roots systems, and they can cause a lot of damage when they fall. We had a tree specialist evaluate the remaining pines on our property to determine how safe they were. One of the pines they wanted to take down was the eagle tree. My husband, Joe, quickly responded, "Not that tree, birds of prey watch for fish from there." Then, a couple of years later, Bounty and Merry chose to build their nest in that very tree!

In 2018, the NC Wildlife Commission came to look at this new nest and their assessment of the tree was that it was better than most. In fact, another eagle tree farther down the Little Tennessee was weak and had fallen into the river. The nest was destroyed. Were Bounty and Merry moving here from that location? The NC Wildlife Commission sent interns down the river in a canoe to see if another nest was being built, but no discovery was made. They also suggested that we not put a camera in or around the nest on our property. That turned out to be wise.

The lay of the land in that field turned out to be a special gift. The field naturally sloped down to the edge of the water from the crest of the hill, where we had a clear view of nest happenings. Much of my free time was spent sitting on a swing at the crest of the hill watching the eagle's nest from January through July each year.

Animal Stories

Photo by Barbara McRae 2019

Photo by Cheryl Binnall 2023

Bounty and Merry and their eaglets acted as if they either did not see me and the many other excited bird watchers and photographers or did not care. But we witnessed time and again that they were and are wonderful parents!

This is a faithful accounting of Merry and Bounty's offspring through the years.

2018	Courageous (Couree) and Daring
2019	Freedom and Ernest (Ernie)
2020	Glory and Hallelujah
2021	Barbara Joy
2022	Keen and Liberty
2023	Majestic and Noble
2024	Orator (Orey) and Patriot (Patty)

A fierce windstorm in December 2023 destroyed their nest. Pictured on the left is a photograph of Bounty and Merry attempting to rebuild in January of 2024. However, in February, they ended up moving back down the river again to a nest they had partially built the year before as a backup. Orator and Patriot hatched at the new nest location in March of 2024 and then fledged in July.

From the six years the eagles nested here, we have many wonderful memories.

Photo by Cheryl Binnall 2024

Animal Stories

Lasting Memories of Merry and Bounty

by Claire Suminski

From the six years Bounty and Merry nested in our field, we have wonderful memories, and we learned many things about American Bald Eagle behavior.

*American Bald Eagles mate for life, but each year, we would catch glimpses of their courtship process. They took turns sitting on their eggs and waiting for them to hatch. Nesting was filled with great suspense for all of us who watched the eagles. We also observed that Merry was about a third bigger than Bounty: it holds true with American Bald eagles that the female is bigger.

*As soon as the eaglets hatched (at 33 to 35 days), and usually before we caught a glimpse of the eaglets, Merry and Bounty would start bringing food to the nest. Mostly fish, but also a variety of snakes and small animals. The parents would rip up the food and feed it to their young. They also cleaned the nest and at times we would find partial carcasses dropped in the field.

*Bounty and Merry carefully guarded the food they harvested by chasing away any competitors: hawks, herons, osprey, otters, beavers and more! Not all competitors left without a fight and some exciting aerial battles ensued! One day, I was working at our home office and a Heron was racing towards the window next to my desk. It avoided collision at the last minute by flying up over the roof, and right behind it was Bounty! Soon after that, one of my neighbors called to report that Merry had tried to drown a heron in the lake. After she flew away, the heron slowly dragged itself onto the shore. The heron lived to see another day!

Animal Stories

*We grind up balsam in the field near the nest for the Balsam Bee project at Cowee School. The balsam is stored in plastic bins during this project. One day I noticed that a movable handle was missing from one of the bins, nowhere to be found on the ground. Later, looking at the nest through binoculars, I clearly saw the handle woven into the structure of the nest. I guess they were paying attention to what we were doing!

* We witnessed a bird birthday celebration when a small flock of white cranes passing by, stopped to perch on the very top of the eagle tree, looking like pretty white birthday candles sticking straight up. The cranes seemed unaware of the eagles and the eagles seemed unaware of them! Would there be a chase or battle? Several minutes passed without incident, before the cranes flew away. Crisis avoided!

*Many bird and nature lovers would stop by to watch and photograph Bounty and Merry and their offspring. A few times we hosted "Breakfast with the Eagles". During one of those events, Barbara Joy (2021: named after Barbara McRae) flew for the first time! And the day our son was married (June 14 ,2020), Glory decided to fledge and gave a short aerial show. These special times are now woven into Suminski family history.

Breakfast with the Eagles 2021 Image made from a photograph taken by Karen Lawrence

*Tragedy struck when Keen (2022) was a new fledgling. He was just becoming acquainted with landing and taking off and was run over by one of our neighbors. A state wildlife officer came to pick up Keen's body. Several of us stood guard in the road for hours, waiting for the officer to arrive. Although Keen's death was profoundly sad, the young eagle had hardly a scratch on him and we were able to see every detail of his body. Over a period of 5 years, eagles' head feathers change to become totally white. Since Keen was in his first year, he was full-size, but without white head feathers. (Young eagles are often wrongly identified because of this.) The wildlife officer took Keen to Balsam, NC to put him in their facility's deep freeze. He was then taken to Raleigh for an autopsy. The report showed he was perfectly healthy! There were no signs of Avian Flu or lead poisoning: two things to watch for in the health of the eagle population.

Keen's feathers were then carefully removed and sent to a feather repository in Colorado for use in Native American celebrations. As sad as his death was, there were resulting benefits.

For now, Bounty and Merry have built another nest downriver. Orator and Patriot hatched in March of 2024 and then fledged in July.

The rest of July was spent practicing hopping and flying around in a nearby field, back and forth with Bounty and Merry close at hand, making occasional food deliveries.

It is always exciting watching the Lake Emory Eagles. Merry and Bounty still come to the tree on our property to fish and hunt and survey their domain. They have mated for life with the dam area as their home place. And we hope they will continue to nest here for years to come.

Animal Stories

My Eagle Watching Journey
FLY EAGLES FLY

by Libby Weber

When I first heard about a nest of eagles on Lake Emory in the spring of 2023, I grabbed my camera and headed out to find it. I didn't know much about the life of an eagle at that time. Little did I know that I would learn a lot from them during the coming months and little did I know that my heart would be stolen by these majestic beauties.

The first time that I saw both adult eagles, America and Bountiful, fly into their nest with food for the eaglets, I was amazed! Never had I seen such grace and precision as they navigated to find the perfect spot to land. They were dropping off their latest kill for their young eaglets, Noble and Majesty.

There was a rivalry between the two eaglets, a rivalry for food. Majesty, being more aggressive of the two got fed first and more often than not, got most of the food brought to the nest. He was quickly growing into the larger of the two. My heart broke for Noble; he tried so hard to be first in line to be fed, but he never achieved victory.

It seemed to me that the only focus for the young eaglets was to eat, sleep and remain safely tucked inside the nest, so that one day they would become strong enough to fly away.

Animal Stories

As they grew and their feathers developed, the eaglets began to venture out onto the limbs, flapping their wings as if pretending to fly. I felt like a nervous parent watching them in fear that they might tumble to the ground.

When first Majesty and then Noble flew away from the nest in late summer to begin their own journey, I was saddened that my early mornings with them had come to an end.

During the months of watching this family of eagles, I experienced an excitement and joy that I can't put into words. I was truly blessed and humbled to have had time with Majesty, Noble, Bountiful and America, and to have witnessed such remarkable creatures.

Pictures by Libby Weber

Animal Stories

An Eagle's Love Story

a poem by Libby Weber

She caught his eyes, He caught hers
While flying in the sky
They became inseparable
And became mates for life
As their bond grew stronger
They built themselves a home
Their union brought a family
One to call their own....
With two eggs in the nest
They sat thru rain and snow
So that the eaglets about to hatch
Protected, would safely grow
Mighty wings capture the wind
Controlling their direction,
No time now for play
Or untimely attention
There are babies on the nest
Mouths you need to feed
Your eaglets must survive
To grow into fledglings
For they have no worries
They watch and sleep and eat
While you soar above the earth
Making meals from what you seek
In time they'll take their place
And soar up in the sky
The cycle will continue
When you've said your last good-bye

Libby Weber
Copyright 2024

Meet North Carolina Wildlife Biologist Chris Kelly

Chris Kelly works for the North Carolina Wildlife Resources Commission. She is passionate about her work. Her home office is based in Asheville, North Carolina, but much of her time is spent travelling around Western North Carolina. Her office is responsible to track and record several different species of animals and birds in this area. And the Biologists sometimes have field technicians that assist them. There is always a lot to do!

Chris has visited our small farm several times because she is helping to track the American Bald Eagle resurgence in Western North Carolina, and their nesting cycles. Chris shared, "We only knew that they start a little later than eagles nesting in the Deep South, and a bit earlier than eagles nesting in the Northeastern US. Now we have some actual dates." She is also compiling dates of nesting milestones from other WNC eagle nests. Chris excitedly reported, "We already have cited two more new eagle nests in Western NC this year! Both are in close proximity to private trout runs." That makes sense because fish is the primary food source of the American Bald Eagles!

It helps Chris and the other Wildlife Biologists when citizens call in to report eagle and nest sightings. They have to cover a lot of ground, so having information regarding a new nest location is very helpful.

Chris has us email her updates regarding the eagles on our property. She is always interested to hear details regarding their behavior and specific nesting progress and dates.

Chris examined the eagles' nest pine tree on our property and found it to be much sturdier than some nest trees she had seen. In fact, she had this to report, "It appears the pair of eagles downstream from you, on Needmore Game Land, lost their nest to a tree falling (or other damage). A former technician, and now volunteer, checked it this week and the nest is gone. We'll be out looking for the pair and a new nest soon. You may see more than two adult eagles passing by your area."

Chris is helping us to be good hosts to the eagles and shares much of her knowledge with us. She shared, "The antics of young birds, especially as they approach fledging, can be quite humorous. It takes them a while to get the hang of handling prey (e.g., plucking fur or feathers, tearing a carcass, not dropping it) and this usually seems to be accompanied by noisy fussing. It sounds like a temper tantrum to our human ears. I'm glad they made it through the intense storms. I worry about raptor nests during rainy springs like the one we've had."
We appreciate Chris, and all that we learn from her!

Animals, Animals, Animals

```
K F L E D G L I N G M G P E O
K I T T E N S C C M E M I B P
A S P O Y B C C A M Q L A I O
N X V F U J I S T S O N T R S
I D O G L N V Z A T E M W D S
M H G Y E S Q U I R R E L S U
A S A L A M A N D E R S R C M
L R H I N C O D O N T Y P U S
S L U G B O B E A R D O K Q K
D G U P N V S F E I G U A N A
S J V G O N C M D O N K E Y D
B C N D D N D G Z L S S E U E
P A H Q P J Y G C V W V L A E
H C L W R A B E X G F X E C R
E O G D C W N D N I Q W Y V N
G S R G E O Y T E A G L E T S
M D J S T A Y K H S P H O L K
Y A R C E K G F K E T N T I D
N S Q M F H J L P F R E X I Z
V V P C S F T J E Q B W K A O
```

The following words can be found going across, down, and diagonally.

ANIMALS
BALD EAGLE
BEAR
BIRDS
CAT
DEER
DOG
DONKEY
EAGLETS
FLEDGLING

HORSE
IGUANA
KITTENS
OPOSSUM
PANTHER
PONY
RHINCODON TYPUS
SALAMANDERS
SQUIRREL

Answers found in the back of the book

It Takes All Kinds of Animals Word Scramble

Unscramble the words below. The first one is partially solved and is a warm-up. If you need some clues look below.

1. BUTYLFTRE   BUTTE____
2. REBA
3. TKIESTN
4. KYODNE
5. HATNREP
6. SOHRES
7. TAEELSLG
8. AANUGSI
9. OMSPSUO
10. ABARORDL

If you need some clues search these pages.
1-pg.26, 2-pg.4, 3-pg.3, 4-pg.17, 5-pg.5, 6-pg.18, 7-pg.30, 8-pg.13, 9-pg.7, 10-pg.22

The answers can be found in the back of this book.

North Carolina Wildlife Resources Commission

FUN FACTS ABOUT THE VIRGINIA OPOSSUM

Scientific Name: Didelphis virginiana
Classification: Game species and furbearer

Opossums have a lower body temperature than most mammals. That makes their bodies more resistant to animal diseases like rabies.

Opossums are nocturnal, which means they are active at night.

In the wild they usually live up to 3 years, but in captivity, they can live for a few more years. This is because there are no predators and they eat a steady diet.

Opossums breed from January to July. They are born after a two week gestation period. These jelly bean sized embryonic young must pull themselves with their forelimbs to the marsupium, or pouch, where they must attach themselves to a nipple in order to survive. Young opossums live in a pouch on their mother's belly until they're too large to fit inside, after which point they will cling to her back.

They can eat thousands of ticks in a week and will also feast on cockroaches, snails, slugs, snakes, mice and rats.

Opossums will go so far as to "play dead" to make a potential predator think they're sick or diseased.

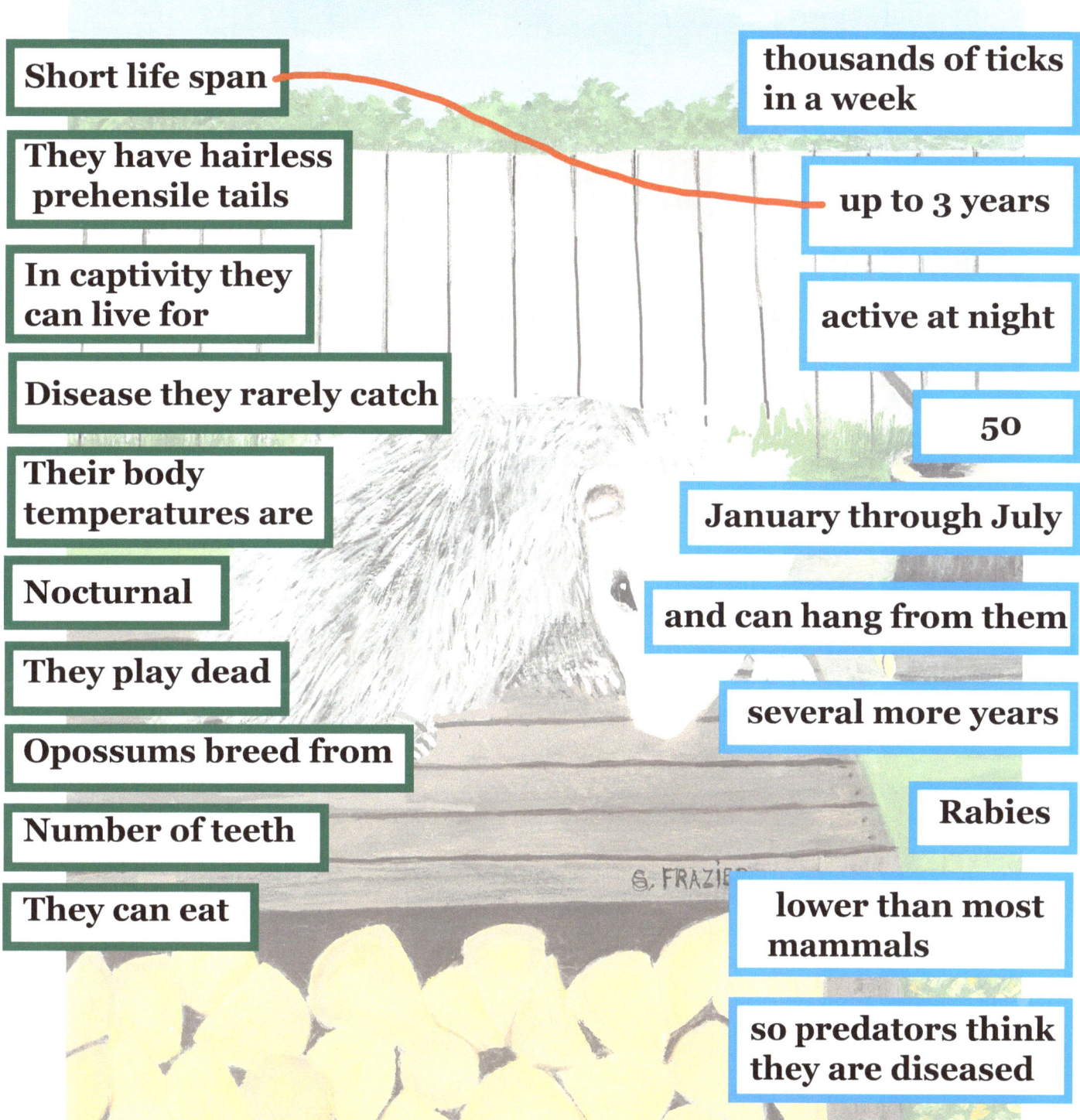

Puzzle Answer Sheet

morning glory
honeysuckle

It Takes All Kinds of Animals Word Scramble

1. BUTYLFTRE — **BUTTERFLY**
2. REBA — **BEAR**
3. TKIESTN — **KITTENS**
4. KYODNE — **DONKEY**
5. HATNREP — **PANTHER**
6. SOHRES — **HORSE**
7. TAEELSLG — **EAGLETS**
8. AANUGSI — **IGUANAS**
9. OMSPSUO — **OPOSSUM**
10. ABARORDL — **LABRADOR**

THE GREAT VIRGINIA OPOSSUM MATCH-UP

Short life span — up to 3 years

They have hairless prehensile tails — and can hang from them

In captivity they can live for — several more years

Disease they rarely catch — Rabies

Their body temperatures are — lower than most mammals

Nocturnal — active at night

They play dead — so predators think they are diseased

Opossums breed from — January through July

Number of teeth — 50

They can eat — thousands of ticks in a week

www.ingramcontent.com/pod-product-compliance
Lightning Source LLC
Chambersburg PA
CBHW061156030426

42337CB00002B/24